The Libertarian Lessons of *South Park*

Libertarianism and Libertarian Philosophy in *South Park*, How Ron Paul, Gary Johnson, and *South Park* Created a New Generation of Libertarians and *South Park* Conservatives

Brandon Simpson

All rights reserved. No portion of this book may be reproduced, transmitted, or stored in whole or in any part by any means, including graphic, electronic, or mechanical without written permission from the author except for the use of brief quotes written in critical articles and reviews.This book has not been approved, endorsed, licensed, or sponsored by any entity or person involved in creating or producing the television series, *South Park*.The images in the *South Park* style are original creations by AnonPaul.

Published by Small Town Press
Dry Ridge, KY

www.smalltownpr.net
www.libertarianforronpaul.com

Editor: Valerie Marie Valentine
http://www.editing-writing.com/marie-valentine/

ISBN-13: 978-09816466-6-4
ISBN-10: 0-9816466-6-2
LCCN: 2013906089

Government is the great fiction through which everybody endeavours to live at the expense of everybody else.

-Frédéric Bastiat

Contents

1 **INTRODUCTION**   1
    What Is a Libertarian?   1
    Liberals and Conservatives and
        Libertarians   4

2 **BUTT OUT**   7
    There Will Be No More Smoking! 11
    The Tyranny of the Majority 13
    Individual Responsibility 14
    Freedom of Choice 15
    Private Property Rights 17

3 **GOO-BACKS**   19
    They Took Our Jobs! 21
    This is America! We Speak English! 23
    Can We Get Rid of all the Mexicans? 26
    Borders and Private Property 28
    The Fence 29
    Nationality 31

4   Gnomes   33

- It's a Capitalist Country! Get Used to It! 34
- The Greedy Small Businessman 35
- The Invisible Gnomes of the Free Market ... 36
- Collect Underpants and Profit 37

5   Something Wall-Mart This Way Comes   39

- Wall-Mart Is Our Neighborhood Friend! 41
- Slave Wages 43

6   Margaritaville   45

- Water and Bread and Margaritas! Yea! 47
- If You Spend It, Goods Will Come! 49
- Heresy Toward the Economy 51
- Public Works 52
- Bail Out the Insurance Company! 54
- Profit & Loss 55
- Aaand It's Gone! 56

7   Go God Go   57

- Science Damn It! 58

8   Medicinal Fried Chicken   61

- Drugs Are Bad, M'Kay? 62
- Finger-Licking Illegal 65

9   Die Hippie Die   67

- Liberal Brainwashing 69

10 ManBearPig — 71
- I'm Super Cereal! — 72

11 Sexual Harassment Panda — 73
- Taxes Make Me a Sad Panda — 74
- Isn't That Fascism? — 75
- There's No Such Thing As a Free Puppy — 76

12 Hooked On Monkey Phonics — 79
- Screw You Guys! I'm Going Home-School! — 80

13 Mr. Hankey the Christmas Poo — 81
- Right Not to Be Offended — 82

14 The Death Camp of Intolerance — 83
- Intolerance Will Not Be Tolerated — 85

15 Reverse Cowgirl — 87
- Last Bastion of American Freedom — 88
- You Can Always Sue Somebody! — 89

16 Douche and Turd — 91
- The Two-Idiot System — 93

17 Other Issues — 97
- I'm Super! Thanks For Asking! — 97
- A 42nd Trimester Abortion — 99
- It's Coming Right For Us! — 101

Respect My *Authoritah!* 102

18 Respect My *Libertah!*   103
I Learned Something Today 103

Recommended Reading   105

Libertarian Websites   107

Chapter 1

Introduction

What Is a Libertarian?

Before we begin analyzing the libertarian lessons of *South Park*, we must first define what a libertarian is. Conservatives believe that libertarians are pot-smoking hippies. Liberals believe that libertarians are either anarchists or corporate tycoons who only care about money. Neither one of these definitions is true. We can define libertarianism with the following two definitions:

1. A libertarian is someone who opposes the initiation of force to achieve political or social goals. (This is the pledge you take when you become a member of the Libertarian Party.)

2. A libertarian is fiscally responsible and socially tolerant. Some say that libertarians are half Democrat and half Republican.

You may notice that I'm spelling libertarian with a lowercase "l." I have to make a distinction between libertarians and Libertarians. A Libertarian is a member of the Libertarian Party. A libertarian is someone who believes in libertarianism, but not necessarily a member of the Libertarian Party. For example, Gary Johnson was a Republican governor of New Mexico, but his policies were very libertarian. He didn't become a Libertarian until he ran for president in 2012.

Another reason that I'm writing libertarian with a lowercase "l" is that I want to compare libertarians to liberals and conservatives, not Libertarians to Democrats and Republicans. I'm also taking into consideration that this book will be read in countries other than the United States, where the same liberal-conservative dichotomy exists.

We also need to define liberal and conservative. A libertarian is fiscally responsible and socially tolerant. A liberal is fiscally irresponsible and socially tolerant. A conservative is fiscally responsible and socially intolerant. In recent years, conservatives have become neoconservatives. Neoconservatives, or neo-cons, are fiscally irresponsible and socially intolerant, the worst of both worlds.

We can also define libertarian with a quote from Andre Marrou, the Libertarian presidential candidate in 1992:

> Liberals want the government to be your mommy. Conservatives want government to be your daddy. Libertarians want it to treat you like an adult.[1]

---

[1] Marrou, Andre. https://www.facebook.com/pages/Andre-Marrou/328460731269?ref=ts&fref=ts

I believe this quote sums up the differences among liberals, conservatives, and libertarians perfectly. Conservatives want to protect you from external enemies like your father would. Liberals want to protect you from yourself like your mother would. Libertarians don't want to be your parents or your nanny. [2]

---

[2]Benedict, Wes. *Introduction to the Libertarian Party*

Liberals and Conservatives and Libertarians

I believe that Matt Stone and Trey Parker have influenced, whether it was their intention or not, a generation of young people to be more libertarian with their show *South Park*. They sum up their political beliefs with the following statement:

> I hate conservatives, but I really fucking hate liberals. [3]

If this book works the way I intend, liberals and conservatives who read it will be libertarians when they finish it. I will use certain episodes as a point of departure to discuss certain issues. In some cases, I will use my experience in France to drive the point further. I will cite some prominent libertarians, but in many cases I don't cite anything. As you read, you will notice that I spend more time trying to convince liberals to be fiscally responsible than I do trying to convince conservatives of being socially intolerant. That is because I believe that fiscal responsibility can be taught more easily than social tolerance. Social intolerance is often motivated by deep religious beliefs, and it is virtually impossible to change one's religious beliefs. For example, Rick Santorum is very conservative, and I don't think anyone can convince him to be socially tolerant. In fact, Santorum recently said that the Republicans are losing elections because they're not anti-gay enough.[4] I'm more optimistic of

---

[3] Leo, Alex. "Matt Stone & Trey Parker Are Not Your Political Allies (No Matter What You Believe)" *Huffington Post*, April, 27 2010, http://www.huffingtonpost.com/2010/02/25/matt-stone-trey-parker-ar_n_475744.html

[4] Terbush, Jon. "Rick Santorum's warning to Republicans: Embracing gay marriage is 'suicidal.'" *The Week*, April 9, 2013, http://theweek.com/article/index/242482/

influencing those who don't feel very strongly about the liberal-conservative dichotomy.

My job in France gave me so much time off that I was able to contemplate the role of government in our lives. And I was able to come to many conclusions, which I discuss in this book, without having read anything about libertarianism beforehand. I used to be liberal, but then I realized that I was a libertarian all along. I just didn't know it.

Each chapter from Chapter Two to Chapter Sixteen is named after an episode from *South Park*. The chapters begin with a description of the episode, in case you haven't seen it. If you're an avid *South Park* fan, you won't need to read these, of course. Some descriptions are longer or shorter than others. The subsequent subsections contain a libertarian lesson from that episode. The episode is used as a point of departure, and there are a few subsections that don't pertain directly to the episode, but rather to the lesson in it. You will notice that a few chapters have more lessons than others. For example, Chapter Two contains many lessons discussed that could easily be discussed in other episodes. While many of the libertarian lessons of *South Park* are often repeated in multiple episodes, each lesson will be discussed only once, but they may be mentioned a few more times.

Before you begin reading, take the world's smallest political quiz to see where you stand politically:

www.theadvocates.org/quiz

Chapter 2

Butt Out

This episode begins with the entire student body of *South Park* Elementary attending an assembly where the presenters are anti-smoking activists. This group, called Butt Out, discusses the dangers of smoking cigarettes to the students through ridiculous dancing and singing. At the end of their presentation, one of the activists tells the students, "If you don't smoke, you can grow up to be just like us!" When the four boys hear this (I will refer to Stan, Kyle, Cartman, and Kenny as the four boys), they don't want to become "lame" like them, so they decide to try smoking cigarettes behind the school. Mr. Mackey, their school counselor, approaches the boys to ask them what they are doing. By this point, the boys have already ditched their cigarettes in the dumpster to avoid being caught. But they have difficulty hiding that they have been smoking because it is difficult for them not to cough and hack. Mr. Mackey concludes that they must have been smoking and starts to tell them the dangers of smoking. During his anti-smoking lecture, the contents of the dumpster catch on fire, which then spreads to the school building, burning the entire thing down. This eventually ends with Shelia Browflowski (Kyle's mom) blaming the tobacco companies for filling the boys' head with propaganda. She doesn't blame the boys for smoking, and she doesn't allow herself, or the other parents to take responsibility for their boys' smoking. She decides to contact an anti-smoking celebrity: Rob Reiner.

The episode cuts away to Rob Reiner's office, where he is reading letters from distraught parents whose children are still smoking, despite his efforts to force people into quitting. His efforts include lobbying to get images of cigarettes removed from films and art, raising taxes on cigarettes, and forcing smokers out of bars and parks. He doesn't understand why people smoke if they know that it's hazardous to their health, while he is eating cheeseburger after cheeseburger (and other fatty, greasy foods). He decides to go to *South Park* and declare war on the tobacco companies.

Reiner arrives in *South Park*, where the whole town has gathered to welcome him. He tells the town that it's good to see so many come together for good health. His plan to take on the tobacco companies is to use the boys, since he believes that the tobacco companies had seduced them into smoking. Reiner and the boys go to a bar-and-grill restaurant where he explains his plan. His plan deals with tricking the tobacco company into letting them in for a school paper and then saying that the tobacco company invited them over in order to seduce them into smoking. Kyle realizes that his plan involves lying, but Reiner believes that his lie is justified since, according to him, the tobacco companies lie about the dangers of smoking. Reiner then smells cigarette smoke coming from a man sitting at the bar. He coughs loudly to try to show the smoker that the smoke is bothering him. The smoker explains to him that he's in a bar, where most people assume and expect that they may smoke. Reiner is shocked to learn that smoking in bars in Colorado isn't illegal. This makes him want to ban smoking in bars in Colorado. Cartman thinks that Reiner is "awesome" because he "just goes around imposing his will on people." Reiner takes the boys to Big Tobacco, the local tobacco company, where he intends to take a picture of the boys so that he can Photoshop it later with cigarettes in their hands. The vicepresident of Big Tobacco, Mr. Harris, gives Reiner and the boys a brief historical tour of tobacco. The history tour concludes with the law that Congress adopted in 1965 that mandated that all tobacco companies put the Surgeon General's warning on their packages. Mr. Harris then tells them, "Everyone knows the dangers of tobacco. But some people still choose to do it, and we believe that's what being an American is all about." Kyle concludes that it is reasonable to allow people to smoke if they are aware of the dangers and still choose to do so. Reiner and the boys see the factory at work with happy factory workers singing about smoking, Reiner takes a photo of the boys in the factory, and then he and the boys flee. They go to a place where Reiner has set up shop to stop smoking. In here, he shows the boys how they get smoking banned by making bogus studies and producing expensive commercials to get the public on their side. Kyle, again, tells him that he's lying. Reiner tells the boys that lying is sometimes okay if you know what's good for people more than they do.

Kyle decides that he's had enough of listening to Rob Reiner and his anti-smoking group. He, Stan, and Kenny decide to leave them alone completely and play, while Cartman agrees to be part of a video that will prove that secondhand smoke can kill you. Little does he know that the anti-smoking people intend to kill him after he records a commercial where he says he'll be dead by the time the commercial will broadcast.

The last scene of the episode takes place at the tobacco company where the vice president and other employees of Big Tobacco have taken Cartman in to protect him from Rob Reiner and his anti-smoking brigade.

There Will Be No More Smoking!

I decided to discuss this episode first because the issue of smoking bans is what made me a libertarian in the first place. Before I discuss this any further, I should mention that I am not a smoker. I have never smoked, and I don't intend to start.

When I was in France, I was shocked to learn that smoking was no longer allowed in bars or restaurants. We all have this image of the French smoking virtually all the time. But in 2008 the French government passed a law that prohibited smoking in public areas like bars and restaurants.[1] This made me think about being a bar owner in America, or more specifically in Kentucky. If I owned a bar, I would never ban smoking, because the majority of bar-goers are probably smokers. If I were a restaurant owner, I would not ban smoking in the entire building, but I would have enough sense to at least have a separate smoking section. There are undoubtedly areas in America where the majority don't smoke and don't want to be around smoke when they're drinking or eating. But what gives these people the right to tell others how to run their business?

I have a friend from England whom we'll call Nigel throughout this book. I told him I would include him in this book and also told him how he would be portrayed. He's particularly left-wing. He jokingly said:

"Ah! Are you going to paint me as a wishy-washy liberal?" I guess I am.

He believes that smoking should be outlawed completely in his country. His reasoning is that he has to pay taxes to support the National Health Service, the United

---

[1] "French Smoking Ban Goes into Effect," January 31, 2007, http://www.drugfree.org/join-together/drugs/french-smoking-ban-goes-into

Kingdom's universal healthcare program (or its system of socialized medicine, if you prefer) and doesn't think he should have to pay for someone's unhealthy habit. This sounds like a good reason to oppose national health insurance. But that's another issue.

Nigel is also a *South Park* fan. When he sees an episode that deals with a conservative or a libertarian point of view, he can somewhat agree with it. But this episode was the big exception. When he watched this episode, I remember his exact words after he finished it:

"I don't think I agree with that!"

The Tyranny of the Majority

If the tyranny of an individual, also known as a monarchy or dictatorship, is wrong, then why is the tyranny of the majority morally better? If one person has the power to declare all rules and laws over the majority of a people without their consent, that person is considered a dictator. If a few people have the power to declare all rules and laws over the majority of a people without their consent, that group of people is also considered dictators. But if the majority of the people have the power to declare all rules and laws over an individual and that individual's place of business, that is called a democracy.

A dictatorship is the tyranny of an individual over the majority. A democracy is the tyranny of the majority over the individual. This is not what a democracy is supposed to be, but voters today believe that a democracy is when the majority makes a rule or law that everyone else has to follow. So, in a way, voters have become dictators. As Paul points out in *Liberty Defined*, democracy "means that the government prevails over the people by claiming the blessing of mass opinion."[2]

---

[2]Paul, Ron. *Liberty Defined* (New York: Grand Central Publishing, 2011), 63-64.

Individual Responsibility

During my teaching assistantship in France, I was asked by one of the teachers what I believed to be the greatest overall difference between Americans and the French. From my point of view, the French believe in social protection, regardless of their political affiliation, and Americans believe in individual responsibility. Or at least we used to.

Individual responsibility is one the basic tenants of libertarianism.[3] This episode touches on individual responsibility. Is it really the government's responsibility to make sure that people don't smoke? Is it the government's responsibility to deny someone the right to make an unhealthy choice? People make hundreds to thousands of choices every day. The choices they make can have positive or negative consequences. In this episode, Rob Reiner believes that it is his responsibility to protect people from smoking because of the dangers it can cause to your health. In the commentary, Stone and Parker say that they think it's ridiculous for a man as fat as Rob Reiner to be worried about his health from secondhand smoke.

Another character who shirks individual responsibility in this episode is Shelia Broflovski (Kyle's mom). Instead of blaming herself and the children, she blames tobacco companies for basically brainwashing the children into wanting to smoke.

---

[3]Rand, Carole Anne. "What Is Libertarianism?" http://www.theadvocates.org/libertarianism-101/definitions-of-libertarianism/

Freedom of Choice

Most of these bans on smoking or trans-fats are motivated by a desire to make people healthier. But living in a free country means that you should have the right to make your own choices. If you're not free to make a poor or unhealthy choice, are you really free? Nobody is forcing you to smoke. Nobody is forcing you to eat a greasy cheeseburger. Nobody is forcing you to consume alcohol. It's all a matter of choice.[4] Remember what Mr. Harris said about tobacco:

> Everybody knows the danger of tobacco. But some people still choose to do it, and we believe that's what being an American is all about.

Another reason to oppose such smoking bans is that it creates a dangerous precedent in which other perceived unhealthy products could be banned. If the government, or the majority of voters, can ban smoking, what would stop them from banning alcohol or fatty foods? Alcohol and fatty foods are bad for your health, so why not ban them as well? Some major cities in America have already banned trans-fats and rare meat in restaurants. Mayor Bloomberg banned Big Gulp cups for soda in New York City 2012.[5] And he recently tried

---

[4] Paul, Ron. *The Revolution* (New York: Grand Central Publishing, 2008), 69, 109.

[5] Gunlock, Julie. "Goodbye Big Gulps In Mayor Bloomberg's New York, Hello Big Government" *Forbes*: http://www.forbes.com/sites/realspin/2012/09/18/goodbye-big-gulps-in-mayor-bloombergs-new-york-hello-big-government/

to ban 2-liter sodas to be delivered with your pizza.[6] Fortunately, a New York judge struck it down.

---

[6]Chasmar, Jessica. "New York Mayor Bloomberg Bans 2-Liter Sodas with Pizza Delivery: report" 24 Feb 2013. Fox News: http://www.foxnews.com/politics/2013/02/25/bloomberg-soda-ban-means-no-2-liter-bottles-with-domino/

Private Property Rights

From my point of view, owning a bar or a restaurant is no different from owning a home. I can allow people to smoke and eat rare burgers in my home, so why can't I do the same thing in my bar or my restaurant?

I would certainly not go to a smoker's home and demand that there be no smoking in his house. The house is his property, and he can do as he pleases. So why should I expect anything different from that person's bar, if he owns one?

Stone and Parker discuss this point of view in the commentary a little bit deeper. And their point of view is that if they want their bar to be a smoking bar, then they should be allowed to do that. They go on to say that they would put up a sign that it's a smoking bar, and if you don't like smoking, then don't go into the bar. The tyranny of the majority does not outweigh the rights of private ownership.

If the government is telling me that I can't allow certain things in my place of business, such as smoking and rare meat, who is the real owner of the business?

One more point I want to make is that you own yourself. Therefore, nobody else can tell you what may or may not go into your body. Libertarianism is the radical notion that other people are not your property.[7]

---

[7] Rothbard, Murray. *For a New Liberty* (Ludwig von Mises Institute, 2002), 22-23.

Chapter 3

Goo-Backs

The episode *Goo-Backs* deals with the issue of immigration. After watching this episode, it appeared to me that Stone and Parker didn't have a very libertarian point of view on immigration. But after listening to the commentary, I realized that they were really just making fun of conservatives who seem to cry out, "They took our jobs!" every three to four years.

This episode starts out with the boys who have start-ed their own snow-shoveling business. After a "shoveling" accident, Cartman needs first aid. The boys go into their client's home and see a news feature that speaks about immigrants who have come from the future looking for work. The future is so overly crowded that there is not enough work to go around.

This leads to more and more immigrants coming from the future, sometimes bringing their entire families with them. Since the immigrants offer to work for such low wages, they get hired all over America. This, of course, causes a problem for the present-day American workers who get laid off.

The displaced workers unite to stop any more immigrants who may come back and take more jobs. Their solutions are ridiculous, such as shooting everyone who crosses the time border and turning gay.

They Took Our Jobs!

In this episode, the immigrants from the future, the *goobacks*,[1] are taking away jobs from present-day Americans. Since they offer to work for such low wages, they are hired all over the country, at the expense of the present-day American workers who are losing their jobs to the immigrants from the future. Nearly everyone is affected, even the boys who had started their snow-shoveling operation. This eventually leads into the meeting of various workers' unions who start yelling one of the most famous lines from *South Park*:

> They took our jobs!

This is clearly an allusion to Mexican immigrants who are accused of taking away jobs from Americans. However, I have not heard of anybody, not even one person, of losing a job to an illegal immigrant. Of course, this is just my personal experience. You may have heard of legitimate stories where an American has lost his job to an illegal immigrant.

Whether this is true or not, let's pretend that illegal immigrants are taking away jobs that could otherwise go to Americans. The first question we need to ask is why an employer would choose to hire an illegal over an American. Most of us already know the answer to this question: Illegal immigrants are willing to work for less, and most Americans refuse to do the hard, back-breaking work that most illegal immigrants are willing to do. If an American were willing to do such work, he would probably demand a wage that the employer simply could not afford. Rand Paul said in a recent interview that most Americans would rather collect government welfare for ten dollars an hour than pick crops

---

[1] This is an obvious reference to the derogatory term "wetback" that is used to refer to Mexicans.

for eight dollars an hour. So this issue of hiring illegal immigrants over Americans is really the free market at work. The employer will pay as little as possible for the most amount of labor he can possibly get.

Here's another question we need to ask: Who's really taking whose job? Of course, the laid-off workers in *South Park* are blaming the immigrants just like many Americans, but they fail to realize who's really taking their jobs. Did those immigrants come, put a gun to their heads, and say, "Give me your job! I'm taking it!" Of course they didn't. It was the employer who took their jobs and then gave them to the immigrants.

Another thing to consider is that some, possibly many, immigrants create their own jobs. For example, how many authentic Mexican restaurants have you seen run by actual Mexicans? In my own town, there is a Mexican restaurant that is operated by Mexicans.[2] Their restaurant created ten to fifteen new jobs, none of which were taken from American workers.[3]

---

[2] I don't know if they're legal or not. I never asked them because it's none of my business.

[3] Paul, Ron. *Liberty Defined*, (New York: Grand Central Publishing, 2011), 150-160.

This is America! We Speak English!

There is a scene in this episode where Mr. Garrison comes into class and announces to the class that he must now teach class in present-day English and Future-Speak. This angers the students, and Kyle says, "This is bullcrap. If they want to live in our time, then they should learn our language."

This particular issue is one that I am particularly passionate about. In fact, I could probably write a whole book based on language policies alone. I can't count the number of times I've heard someone, usually a stubborn conservative, say "This is America! We speak English!" The liberal stance on language policy is that people should be allowed to speak whichever language they want, but they also believe in using politically correct terminology. Conservatives believe you should be free to say whatever you want, as long as you say it in English.

Before I continue, I need to mention that, contrary to popular belief, there is no official, or mandatory, language in the United States. During the Republican debates, I remember that Newt Gingrich, among other candidates, was in favor of making English the official language. When they say official language, I think they really mean mandatory language. They want to declare a language that everyone must speak, which is English. I can think of at least three reasons why libertarians should oppose declaring a mandatory language.

The first reason, and often the most overlooked, is that declaring a mandatory language would contradict the free speech provision in the first amendment of the Constitution. The second reason is that it violates the primary definition of libertarianism: the initiation of force to achieve a political or social goal. And declaring a mandatory language is, without a doubt, force.

The third reason to oppose mandatory languages is that language itself is a product of the free market. I've studied several languages and majored in Spanish and French, and I had never considered that languages were products of the free market until I read Milton Friedman's *Free to Choose*. In his book, Friedman says that the language we speak was not ordered into creation from a government bureau. It was created by voluntary individuals who were willing to communicate with one another. If we oppose competing languages, we are in fact opposing the free market.[4]

One common argument I hear from the pro-English advocates is that immigrants won't assimilate or be successful in America if they don't learn English. This is pure nonsense. Immigrants already understand the importance of learning English, and no amount of legislation will change that. And the transition from the native language to English usually occurs in three generations. Typically, the first generation speaks the native language well and tries to learn English as quickly as possible. Their children, the second generation, will grow up speaking the native language at home, but they will eventually learn English from their neighbors and friends at school. In fact, their English will usually turn out better than their native language since they are being educated in English. By the time the third generation, the grandchildren of the original immigrants, arrives, the transition from the native language to English is complete. This generation will more than likely speak English only.

Declaring a mandatory language also sets the precedence of establishing a language bureau, a Department of the English Language, if you will. Such a depart-

---

[4]Friedman, Milton. *Free to Choose*, (New York: Houghton Mifflin Harcourt Publishing Company), 25.

ment could easily establish standards to the English language spoken in America, which would be taught in our schools. You may think that this sounds absurd and far-fetched, but keep in mind that France has an organization similar to this: the French Academy, or the Académie Française, in French. This organization was established to be the authority on the usages of grammar and vocabulary in the French language. Recently, the French Academy has tried to prevent the inclusion of English words in the French language, which I believe is completely futile.

But what if a language bureau succeeded in defining or replacing words? Although I can't find any evidence of this, I have suspected the French Academy of promoting the word *contribuable*, which translates as *taxpayer*. However, the word *contribuable* literally means *contributor*. But we all know that contributions are voluntary, not coerced like taxes are. So why would the word *contribuable* be used? My only assumption is that people feel better paying taxes if they're labeled as contributors, even without realizing that they're actually being coerced into paying taxes.[5]

Conservatives want to keep the government out of our wallets, but why do they want the government in our dictionary? Do they not see that this could lead to a *1984* scenario in which the government publishes the only dictionary allowed for public use? A dictionary that contains words deemed only by the government's authority?

---

[5]On a personal note, I absolutely hate translating the word *taxpayer* to *contribuable* in French.

Can We Get Rid of all the Mexicans?

Conservatives typically oppose free immigration, while liberals support it. In this episode, Daryl Weathers, also known as Pissed-Off White Trash Redneck Conservative, believes that the time border should be closed to future immigrants in order to prevent more job losses. On the other side of the argument is Aging Hippie Liberal Douche, who first calls Weathers an ignorant redneck like most liberals would, who believes that the immigrants have every right to be here. He also explains to Pissed-Off Redneck that his ancestors were also immigrants and that denying these immigrants access to our country would be hypocritical.

The reason that conservatives oppose it is that it is impossible to have free immigration and a welfare state. We had free immigration before 1914, and if you ask anyone if they think that this was good, they will more than likely say it was. If you ask anyone if they think free immigration is good nowadays, they will definitely say no. Milton Friedman asked this question of his audience during a lecture on illegal immigration, and his audience came to the same conclusion. So, without a welfare state, we would have the right kind of immigration. We would have immigrants who come here to work, not to be a drain on a welfare state.[6]

In a recent interview, Senator Rand Paul discussed the illegal immigration issue that we have today. He confirmed what I already believed to be true: illegal immigrants do not collect welfare benefits. They can't exploit the welfare system because they are not citizens. Friedman mentioned this as well thirty years ago. Friedman said that immigration is good as long as it's illegal,

---
[6]Paul, Ron. *Liberty Defined*, (New York: Grand Central Publishing, 2011), 150-160.

which is a strange paradox. If immigrants are illegal, they can't reap the benefits of the welfare state. If they are legal, they can.[7]

---

[7] Friedman, Milton. "Milton Friedman - Illegal Immigration - PT 1" https://www.youtube.com/watch?v=3eyJIbSgdSE

Borders and Private Property

In a way, denying someone to immigrate can be a violation of private property rights. Does the government own your land? Or do you own your land? Does the government own your business? Or do you own your business? If you own your land and your business, then you are the one who can decide whether or not a person may venture onto your property.

The border between two countries is just an invisible line. The border between your yard and your neighbor's yard is just as invisible. Let's pretend that you own some land where the southern border is also the border between Mexico and the United States. If someone from Mexico wanted to come onto your land, what right would the government have to tell you that you couldn't let them?

We've already established that this would violate the rights of private ownership. If the government can tell you that you are not allowed to have certain people on your property, you do not actually own your property. The government owns it. In this sense, the government is taking the role of a parent who tells his children that they can't hang out with certain other children.[8]

---

[8] Paul, Ron. *Liberty Defined*, (New York: Grand Central Publishing, 2011), 150-160.

The Fence

During the workers' meeting, all the laid-off workers are trying to figure out a way to stop more immigrants from coming. Their first solution is to shoot everyone who crossed the time border, but this idea is rejected by their congressman. The next proposed solution is to create more global warming, but this idea is also rejected on the grounds that it doesn't exist and, if it did exist, it would take too long to occur. The last solution they think of is to "get gay with each other." The laid-off workers believe that having gay sex with each other will prevent the future from happening. If they're not reproducing, then there will be nobody from the future to take their jobs.

I don't think Stone and Parker meant for this to have any symbolic meaning, but I was able to see some symbolism here. The idea of having gay sex to prevent immigration from the future is ridiculous. And many of the proposed solutions to stop immigration from Mexico and other countries are also ridiculous.

The most popular proposed solution is to build a fence between the United States and Mexico. However, the fence is easily penetrable. On Penn and Teller's program *Bullshit*, Penn Jillette hired six illegal immigrants to build a fence. These particular illegal immigrants had already built part of the fence between Mexico and the United States.[9] It took them eight hours to build it. After they had finished building it, they were instructed to get around the fence. The six were split into three teams. One team had to climb over the fence. One team had to go under the fence. And the last team had to go through the fence. All three teams had got around the fence in

---

[9] That's right. The fence is being built by illegal immigrants.

less than ten minutes. The fence they built was just like the fence that was being built along the border. [10]

During the Republican debates, Ron Paul said on numerous occasions that building a fence or a wall along the border was dangerous to liberty. If a wall can keep people out, then it can also be used to keep people in. This type of wall would be similar to the Berlin Wall that separated the capitalist West Germany and the communist East Germany. [11]

The most ridiculous solution I have ever heard to stop immigration is to fill the Rio Grande with alligators. I heard this on the *Daily Show with Jon Stewart*. One of the correspondents, Asif Mandvi, interviews two American citizens who are trying to defend the border. One of the border guards recommends filling the Rio Grande with alligators. However, the other border guard had already looked into this possibility and discovered that filling the Rio Grande with alligators is illegal.[12]

---

[10] "Immigration." Penn & Teller: Bullshit!, Showtime. 26 Apr. 2007.
[11] "Ron Paul Says The Border Fence Built To Keep Us In," http://www.youtube.com/watch?v=esp-ruhkZqQ
[12] "Episode March 30, 2009, The Daily Show, Comedy Central" http://www.thedailyshow.com/watch/mon-march-30-2009/borderline-cops

Nationality

Although this episode doesn't address the issue of nationality, I would like to offer a libertarian point of view on it. What is nationality? Basically, you're assigned a nationality at birth. If you're born in America, you're American. If you're born in Mexico, you're Mexican. If you're born in France, you're French. You get the idea.

However, nationality is a collectivist concept. And most libertarians reject collectivism. By nature, libertarians are very individualistic and don't like to be labeled as if they belong to a certain group.

Another point of view that is often overlooked is that nationality is really assigned by the government. But what right does the government have to assign you a nationality? As a child, you are too young to know which nationality you want to have, if any.

Chapter 4

Gnomes

The episode "Gnomes" starts out with Mr. Garrison giving his students an assignment on a current event. The boys are assigned to work with Tweek, a nervous and jittery boy whose father has a coffee shop in town. Tweek says they should write about the gnomes that come into your room and steal your underpants. They spend the night at Tweek's house to see these gnomes, but they fail to see them.

Mr. Tweek had already written a presentation for them about corporate takeovers ruining America. He wants to use the children to get the public on his side so that he can get rid of Harbuck's Coffee, a big coffee corporation.

The owner of Harbuck's, John Postem, had already offered Mr. Tweek $500,000 to buy out his coffee shop, but Mr. Tweek refuses his offer.

The episode ends with the boys reading a presentation about the benefits of corporations like Harbuck's Coffee. Harbuck's stays, and the gnomes continue to steal people's underpants.

It's a Capitalist Country! Get Used to It!

In this episode, the owner of Harbuck's Coffee, John Postem, offers to buy Mr. Tweek's coffee shop for $500,000. Mr. Tweek refuses the offer and tells Postem that his coffee shop isn't for sale. In response to this, Postem tells Mr. Tweek that he'll have to build his Harbuck's right next door. Mr. Tweek laments to Postem that doing that can put him out of business. Postem's reply is, "This is a capitalist country. Get used to it!"

This type of scenario has happened numerous times all across America. A big company comes into town and drives the smaller companies out of business. People will often blame the big companies for destroying the small ones. However, people fail to realize that the consumers drive out the small companies. The big companies, be it a coffee shop or a grocery store, can usually sell their merchandise for less money than the small companies can. And consumers will almost always choose to spend less money if they are able. Why would you spend four dollars at a small coffee shop when you can get the same coffee for three dollars at the big coffee shop?[1]

---

[1] Paul, Ron. *The Revolution*, (New York: Grand Central Publishing, 2008), 69-108.

The Greedy Small Businessman

In this episode, we see that corporations are not the only ones that will use underhanded tricks to get an edge on their competition. Mr. Tweek tries to sell himself as a small business owner who sells "simple coffee for a simpler America." Instead of relying on the quality of his product, he enlists the help of the local government to protect him from what he sees as unfair competition.

The boys need to write a presentation on a local event for their class. Tweek suggests that they write about the underpants gnomes, but since the four boys don't see the gnomes, they accept a presentation from Mr. Tweek that was written about corporate takeovers. Mr. Tweek intends to use the children to pull at the people's heartstrings to get Harbuck's coffee out of town.

The boys have to do another presentation in front of everyone in town. This time they actually see the gnomes, who agree to teach them about businesses and corporations. In their newly written speech, they tell the people of *South Park* that corporations are good. Without corporations, we wouldn't have access to cars, computers, and other products. The boys continue on to say that even Harbuck's started out as a small business that eventually grew into the giant corporation it is today.[2]

---

[2]Paul, Ron. *The Revolution*, (New York: Grand Central Publishing, 2008), 69-108.

The Invisible Gnomes of the Free Market

Paul Cantor wrote in an article about this episode that the gnomes are normally invisible and only come out at 3:30 in the morning. He believes that the gnomes represent the invisible hand of the free market that Adam Smith describes in his book *The Wealth of Nations*. He suggests that most people don't even see the economic activity taking place right in front of their eyes. Or they fail to notice or understand it.[3]

I'm a small businessman myself. Although I work in the publishing industry, I don't fully understand how it works. Technically, I'm a small self-publisher. I know that after submitting my book files to my printer, my book will become available on Amazon.com and also available to some bookstores, but I don't fully understand the intermediary process. This is another example of the invisible hand of the free market at work.

---

[3]Cantor, Paul. *South Park and Philosophy*, (Oxford: Blackwell Publishing, 2007), 97-111.

Collect Underpants and Profit

When the gnomes try to explain their business plan to the boys, they seem to not understand their own plan. Phase One of their plan is to collect underpants. Phase Three is profit. But Phase Two has a giant question mark. I never understood the meaning behind this until I read Cantor's article.

According to Cantor, this business plan with a question mark in the middle represents the economic illiteracy of the average American. Most Americans can't see the connection between the activities of businessmen and the profits they make. He goes on to say that most would rather complain about the obscene profits that corporations make.[4]

Cantor also says that the gnomes' business plan represents the lack of financial literacy of many businessmen. Again, my lack of understanding of how the entire publishing business operates is a good example. I know that I will eventually turn a profit from my books, but I don't know how the entire intermediary process works. For me, Phase One is to write a book. Phase Two is a question mark. And Phase Three is profit.[5]

---

[4]Cantor, Paul. *South Park and Philosophy* (Oxford: Blackwell Publishing, 2007), 97-111.

[5]For the record, I have read many books about the publishing industry.

Chapter 5

Something Wall-Mart This Way Comes

"Something Wall-Mart This Way Comes"[1] deals with Wal-Mart[2] and its effects on small towns. It begins with the opening of a new Wall-Mart, where the entire town has gathered to rejoice in its arrival.

Once the people of *South Park* begin to shop at Wall-Mart, the small shops on Main Street start to lose business and are forced to close their doors. Kyle tries to get the town to stop shopping at Wall-Mart by showing them the consequences of doing so. The people of the town agree to stop shopping there, but in the end they can't resist Wall-Mart's low prices.

The boys go to Bentonville, Arkansas to learn how to stop Wall-Mart. They meet one of the creators of the Wall-Mart Super Center, who tells them that they can destroy Wall-Mart by destroying its heart, which is located in the television department. The boys head

---

[1] The title of this episode is a spoof of the horror novel by Ray Bradbury *Something Wicked This Way Comes*.
[2] Wal-Mart refers to the actual Wal-Mart. Wall-Mart refers to the Wall-Mart in the show.

back to *South Park*. Stan and Kyle locate the heart of the *South Park* Wall-Mart, a mirror, and destroy it. Destroying the mirror causes the Wall-Mart to implode and evaporate into oblivion.

Now that the Wall-Mart is gone, the people of *South Park* decide to shop at one store, which turns into a major department store like Wall-Mart.

Wall-Mart Is Our Neighborhood Friend!

For as long as I can remember, there was a simple Wal-Mart in my hometown. It didn't offer groceries. It only sold clothes, toys, and other household items. In the late '90s, however, this Wal-Mart moved to a different location, closer to the interstate highway, and became a Super Wal-Mart. People could shop for clothes and groceries at the same time.

What affect did this have on the other smaller businesses? The presence of this bigger Wal-Mart eventually drove out the small grocery stores. People are quick to blame Wal-Mart for this, but is it really Wal-Mart's fault?

Before the Super Wal-Mart, we had an IGA, a Food Lion, and other various grocery stores across the county. The IGA quickly went under after the Super Wal-Mart came to town. The little Food Mart in Williamstown went out of business shortly after. And many of the small businesses on Main Street also went out of business.

People will focus on what they can see. They can see the correlation between Wal-Mart's presence and the small business failures. But they fail to see why Wal-Mart's presence is putting the small stores out of business. Is Wal-Mart physically forcing these stores out? Of course not. But most would see it that way. If Wal-Mart isn't the reason, what is?

Consumerism is the reason. Wal-Mart can offer to sell their goods for less money than the small stores can. If a person can buy the same product for less money at another store, that person will buy that product at the other store. We saw this phenomenon in Gnomes. Since the majority of consumers choose to spend less money at Wal-Mart, they aren't spending their money at the local stores on Main Street. This is the reason that small businesses go under when a Wal-Mart comes into town.

After listening to the commentary of this episode, I found out that Stone and Parker don't believe Wal-Mart to be an evil being the way they portrayed it *South Park*. They were really just satirizing how many people in America do believe that Wal-Mart is an evil being. Their stance is simple: If you don't like Wal-Mart, then don't go![3] In this episode, Kyle told everyone that Wall-Mart wasn't evil and that everybody just needed to have a little personal responsibility and not shop at Wall-Mart.

Toward the end of the episode, Stan and Kyle were told that they had to destroy the heart of Wall-Mart to get rid of it. They find the heart of Wall-Mart, which was really just a mirror. The mirror shows them that the real heart of Wall-Mart is the consumer. If they want Wall-Mart to "die," the consumers have to stop shopping there.

---

[3]Parker & Stone. "Something Wall-Mart This Way Comes | Commentary (South Park)" http://www.youtube.com/watch?v=SGfGXNsWyW0

Slave Wages

I've heard many liberals complain that Wal-Mart doesn't pay its employees wages that they can live on. And that's one of the reasons that they refuse to shop there.

Contrary to popular belief, Wal-Mart pays its employees more than minimum wage. The current minimum wage is $7.25 an hour. I have never heard of any Wal-Mart employee earning less than $8.00 an hour. And Wal-Mart, along with other companies, is in favor of raising the minimum wage. Wal-Mart supported that last minimum wage increase from $5.15 an hour to $7.25 an hour. And Wal-Mart is already set to support another increase from $7.25 an hour to $9.00 an hour.[4]

Why would Wal-Mart willingly support a law that would make them pay more than they need to? According to academic studies, employees are less likely to quit their jobs when they are paid more and that they will spend more money, and therefore be better consumers.[5] If Wal-Mart and other businesses want to keep their good employees from quitting, they can very well pay them more without a government mandate. So why would Wal-Mart support the mandate at all?[6]

The answer to this question is very simple. Wal-Mart doesn't want to raise the minimum wage to give its employees a higher wage or to prevent them from quitting. Wal-Mart, along with other businesses, is

---

[4]Prime, Peter. "New York Minimum Wage Laws: Lessons for the Rest of the Nation" *PolicyMic*:http://www.policymic.com/articles/31355/new-york-minimum-wage-law-lessons-for-the-rest-of-the-nation

[5]Did we really need an academic study to know this?

[6]Prime, Peter. "New York Minimum Wage Laws: Lessons for the Rest of the Nation" *PolicyMic*:http://www.policymic.com/articles/31355/new-york-minimum-wage-law-lessons-for-the-rest-of-the-nation

in favor of raising the minimum wage to destroy its competition. Wal-Mart knows that the small shops and grocery stores on Main Street can't afford to pay their employees the federally mandated minimum wage. This means the owners of small businesses have to either let some of their employees go, or they will be forced to shut their businesses down.

Advocates of the minimum wage fail to see its negative effects. The minimum wage can cause small businesses to go under. It can also cause higher unemployment. If a prospective employee is trying to procure a job for which the minimum wage is $9.00, the employer has to determine if that person's skills justify such a wage. If said applicant has experience in that employer's industry, the employer is more compelled to hire him. If, however, said applicant has no experience in the employer's industry, the employer will be reluctant to hire him and will wait until another applicant with the necessary skills applied for the position. The alternative to a low wage is unemployment.[7]

So, the minimum wage law really says that employers must discriminate against those whose skills don't justify such a wage. I'm sure you've heard of job seekers complaining that they can't find work because they lack the necessary experience and that they can't gain the experience if nobody hires them. As you can see from the above explanation, the minimum wage law is a big reason behind this. The minimum wage law really protects skilled workers from perceived unfair competition from unskilled workers.

---

[7] Hazlitt, Henry. *Economics in One Lesson* (New York: Three Rivers Press, 1979), 134-139.

Chapter 6

Margaritaville

Margaritaville deals with the financial crisis that occurred in 2008. It begins in a bank where Stan is depositing $100 that he received from his grandmother. Stan wants to spend it, but his father Randy wants him to learn the importance of saving. He deposits the $100 into a new bank account, and then loses it. More people lose their money, and more people lose their jobs because there's no money.

Stan asks his father why there is suddenly no money, but Randy doesn't really understand why. He believes that frivolous spending has angered the economy, as if the economy were some omnipotent being. He does, however, convince the rest of the town that frivolous spending is the reason for the financial crisis. And the rest of the town follows his lead of not spending hardly a dime, hoping that the economy will return to them.

Kyle presents a different path. Kyle believes that spending is good for the economy. This leads the savers (Randy's entourage) to believe he is either a heretic or the economy's "son" to save them.

Kyle gets a credit card with no spending limit and pays for everyone's debts. The newly debt-free people of *South Park* start to spend once more.

Water and Bread and Margaritas! Yea!

Randy exemplifies people's priorities when they need to save money. He has the right idea: save money, spend less. Contrary to what mainstream economists like Paul Krugman believe, saving is the engine of economic growth, not spending. Randy, however does what many people do when they try to save money. He confuses his needs with his desires. People need water and food, but nobody needs margaritas.

George Clason describes this type of confusion in his book *The Richest Man in Babylon*. The character in this book, Arkad, is teaching the people of Babylon how to become wealthy themselves. He gives them seven cures to a lean purse. The first two cures are to save ten percent of your income and to control your expenses. His students lament that it is impossible to save ten percent of their incomes. They needed to spend all of it. Arkad tells them that their "necessary expenses" will always grow to equal their incomes unless they acknowledge that certain "necessities" are actually "desires."[1] What kind of "necessities" are actually "desires" in present-day America? I remember when my old television set broke a few years ago. It was a minor inconvenience to me, but my mother said, "You need a TV!" In her mind, and in the minds of many, a television has become a "necessity." But nobody really needs a television. A television can't put food in your mouth or money in your pocket.

If people changed their spending habits and withheld gratification, they could become wealthy as well. It's as easy as saving ten percent of your income. If you're worried that you will spend more than ninety

---

[1] Clason, George. *The Richest Man in Babylon*. (New York: Penguin Group), 41.

percent of your income, put that ten percent aside somewhere before you spend the rest.

If You Spend It, Goods Will Come!

Mainstream economists today believe that consumer spending drives the economy. This idea was popularized by John Maynard Keynes, a British economist who believed that saving money was detrimental to the economy. His view was that the money needed to circulate to have a healthy economy and that the state would have to sometimes step in to fix it. He called it the paradox of thrift. Keynes's book *The General Theory* gave the governments of the world a scientific rationale for doing what they wanted to do anyway. They wanted to expand the power of their governments by removing the barriers that the free market places on them.[2]

We've already established that saving money grows the economy, so why do so many buy into the idea of spending money? My only assumption is that spending is easier than saving for most people today. But how can we tell which is better for the economy? The answer to this is surprisingly simple. If it works at the individual level, it will also work at the group level (or government level).

I can use a personal story to drive my point further. A few years ago, I was in fairly deep credit card debt. I had three credit cards, all of which were maxed out. One day I received a phone call from a collections agent. I was behind on one of my payments. I don't know what compelled me to do this, but it was that moment that made me decide to pay off my credit cards and be out of debt once and for all. If Keynesianism were right, I should have been living well. If I'm in that much debt, I had to have spent a lot first. But all that spending didn't

---

[2]Paul, Ron. *Liberty Defined.* (New York: Grand Central Publishing, 2011), 166-177.

help me personally. It just left me in debt with hardly anything to show for it.

Over the next few months, I kept track of every single penny I spent. I forwent eating out at restaurants. When I did go out to eat, I asked for a free water and ordered the cheapest thing on the menu. I sold half my DVD collection online to generate more money, and I also worked two jobs. After six months, I had paid off $3,000 worth of credit card debt.

I was very proud of myself for doing this. But then another thought hit me. If I hadn't been in debt, I could've saved $3,000 or possibly more given that I wouldn't have had to pay off the high interest rates. The money I saved could've been used to reinvest in my publishing business.

The people of *South Park* in this episode were in a financial kerfuffle. Almost all of them were following Randy's advice of saving money. Kyle, on the other hand, told people that spending money was fine. But the people of *South Park* couldn't, or wouldn't, spend their money. They were all in deep debt. It wasn't until Kyle paid for everyone's debt that the economy of *South Park* started to recover.

Of course, Randy doesn't learn his lesson. After his debt is paid off, he buys another Margaritaville mixer with more advanced features. "We need this!" he says to himself.

Heresy Toward the Economy

Later in the episode, Kyle explains to the people of South Park that faith is the reason an economy exists. The economy has failed because people have lost their faith in it.

This is actually very close the real truth behind our financial system. Since 1971, we have been on fiat money standard, not a gold standard. Some people believe that we're still on a gold or silver standard, but we're not. If you don't know what the gold standard is, it is a system where the banknotes in your wallet would be redeemable for gold. But since we're no longer on a gold standard, the banknotes in your wallet have value only because you believe they do. And since 1971, politicians and the Federal Reserve have been able to print as much as they wanted to spend.

That's why we've had inflation. People have come to believe that inflation is higher prices. But higher prices are the result of inflation, not the definition of it. Inflation is an increase in the money supply. Without a gold standard to keep the Federal Reserve in check, inflation will continue to drive prices up.[3]

---

[3]Schiff, Peter. *The Real Crash.* (New York: St Martin's Press, 2012), 106-125.

Public Works

Some people will cry out that the government can create public works programs that keep people employed. It doesn't matter what the employee is doing, as long as they are receiving a salary that they can spend. That's the purpose of public works programs: to increase spending. But we've already established that this is an economic fallacy.

If these same people had productive jobs, they would still be spending their money and there would also be more products to go around. When there are more products available, be it more television sets or more cars, the price of those products will go down.

One hundred percent of income earners, whether they are producers or bureaucrats, will be on the consuming side of the equation. But if only sixty percent of those income earners are on the producing side, they have to produce for one hundred percent of the people. This means that the price of the products will be higher than they should be.[4]

When I was in France, I worked as an English-language assistant. Officially, I worked twelve hours per week and received about €1,000 a month. But in reality, I only worked thirty minutes a week. And other assistants reported that their teachers weren't even using them. To top it off, the school I worked in provided its assistants with free housing. I received a check from the French government, and I lived in a school dorm without having to pay rent. This situation was the closest that I have ever been to being on welfare.

Liberals would say that my situation wasn't that bad. But they fail to see the underlying problem. Yes, I

---

[4]Hazlitt, Henry. *Economics in One Lesson*, (New York: Three Rivers Press, 1979), 31-36.

was receiving a salary that I could then spend. But I wasn't producing anything that would benefit the French economy. I was really being subsidized by the taxpayers of France.[5]

---

[5]Hazlitt, Henry. *Economics in One Lesson*, (New York: Three Rivers Press, 1979), 37-39.

Bail Out the Insurance Company!

At the end of the episode, Stan finally has the chance to return his father's Margaritaville mixer and get a refund. He presents his problem to a financial committee in Washington. The men of the committee determine his mixer's value at $90 trillion. Stan, of course, is completely confused and surprised by this. He goes into the chamber of the financial committee to see how they determine what action to take.

There is a large round structure, like a skating rink, with several labels such as "Bailout," "Tax the Rich," "Indian Casino," "$1 Billion," and so on. In order to determine the necessary action in response to an economic dilemma, the members of the financial committee take a live chicken, chop its head off, and then let the body run around the circle until it falls. The label it falls on is the action that the financial committee takes.

I think that this scene represents the absolute futility of government intervention in the economy. No action it takes, regardless of how it came to decide them, will help or improve the economy. The government's actions can actually make matters worse.[6]

Kyle's paying for everyone's debts was an obvious allegory to Jesus Christ dying for everyone's sins. But Kyle can also represent the American taxpayer who has to pay when some other person or group is bailed out. In this case, he more or less bailed out the entire town by paying for their debts.

---

[6]Paul, Ron. *Liberty Defined* (New York: Grand Central Publishing, 2011), 168.

Profit & Loss

Since we just saw the negative effects of a bailout on the American taxpayer, let's discuss the capitalist system a little further. In an interview with Phil Donahue, Milton Friedman discussed why the American taxpayer should not be bailing out Chrysler.[7]

According to Friedman, capitalism is not a profit system. It's a profit-and-loss system. Losses are just as important, or even more, in a free market economy. Losses eliminate inefficient, poorly managed businesses. If a company is losing money, that company has to do something to stop losing money and start accumulating money. If the company receives a government bailout, the problem that created the losses is still present in the company. And the only way to eliminate the problem is to allow the company to fail.[8]

After Kyle bailed out the entire town, there was one person who hadn't learned his lesson: Randy. After having his debt paid off, Randy buys another Margaritaville mixer that he probably couldn't afford. Since he can't afford it, he may end up in deep debt yet again. And he may expect another bailout yet again. Randy represents the irresponsible, money-losing company who gets bailed out and winds up in the same position as before his bailout.

---

[7]Friedman, Milton. "Milton Friedman on Bailouts" http://www.youtube.com/watch?v=be5Ty5tP8us

[8]Friedman, Milton. *Free to Choose*, (New York: Houghton Mifflin Harcourt Publishing Company, 1980), 45.

Aaand It's Gone!

Once Stan deposits his money, the bank loses it in a flash. I think this symbolizes the truth behind many businesses and financial institutions today. And the truth is that many people and businesses don't really have any money at all. They all have debts to one another.

After reading books and watching videos about the 2008 financial crisis, it became clear that the reason behind the crisis was that there was too much debt. As long as everyone continues paying, the debt circle can live. But if one person or party stops paying, the entire debt-financed system will collapse.

As Daniel Hannan, a Member of European Parliament, so eloquently stated:

> The elemental cause of our discontent is easily stated. There's too much debt.[9]

---

[9] Hannan, Daniel. "You can't stave off the hangover by staying drunk" http://www.youtube.com/watch?v=J52BQFdPLJ4

Chapter 7

Go God Go

"Go God Go" is two-part episode that deals with atheism, Richard Dawkins and his book *The God Delusion*, and the teaching of evolution in public schools.

It begins with Mrs. Garrison's refusal to teach evolution to her students because she believes that evolution is a myth.[1] Mrs. Garrison is forced to teach evolution anyway, but she doesn't teach it properly, so the school enlists the help of Richard Dawkins, an evolutionary biologist, to teach evolution to the students.

Another subplot of the episode is Cartman's impatience for the new Nintendo Wii. In the commentary of this episode, Stone and Parker said that Cartman's impatience reflected their own impatience. They spent 5% of the day reflecting religion and spent the other 95% of the day thinking about the Wii.

According to Dawkins, there would be no war without religion. But when Cartman freezes himself and is revived five hundred years in the future, there are three atheist groups, all of whom are at war with one another.

---

[1] By this point in the series, Mr. Garrison has had a sex-change operation.

Science Damn It!

Believing in one religion or another isn't really a libertarian issue. There are libertarian Christians, libertarian Jews, and even libertarian atheists. And I would like to offer my two cents on atheists.

Atheists, for the most part, are extremely liberal. They tend to vote for Democratic candidates because they believe voting for a candidate who doesn't believe in evolution is embarrassing.[2] I would like to pose a question to any liberal atheist reading this right now: If Barack Obama came out and said that he believed in creationism without altering his other beliefs, would you still vote for him?

Let's pretend a little further. If Barack Obama believed in creationism and John McCain believed in evolution, while their other political positions remained the same, would you vote for John McCain instead of Barack Obama?

I've read on many message boards and forums where liberals say they would never vote for Ron Paul because he doesn't believe in evolution. But what difference does it make what a candidate believes so long as he doesn't enforce his beliefs on others? That's more important than his beliefs. Whether a candidate believes in evolution or creationism isn't the problem. The problem arises when they try to enforce their beliefs on other people through legislation. A fascist evolutionist is just as bad as a fascist creationist.[3]

Unfortunately, liberals have a monopoly on the atheist voting bloc. But I think atheists should be libertarian. Atheists reject the notion that an all-powerful supreme

---

[2] Most Republican candidates don't believe in evolution.
[3] Paul, Ron. *Liberty Defined*, (New York: Grand Central Publishing, 2011), 104-107.

being is watching them or controlling their lives. If atheists reject that notion, why would they willingly subject themselves to being watched and controlled by mere mortal men?

Not believing in God or a supreme being is one thing. It is entirely another thing to believe that you are God. What do liberals try to do? They try to create a utopian society for people to live in. In other words, they're trying to create Heaven on Earth. But doesn't the initiation of force undermine the concept of utopia in the first place?

This episode also shows the ostensible reasons for which people go to war. In his book, Dawkins believes that there would be no war if religions were absent. But Stone and Parker show that the three atheist groups of the future are indeed at war with one another. The reason that they are at war is extremely petty: They disagree on what to call themselves. This just goes to show that adherents of any ideological movement, even supposedly rational atheists, can get more caught up in symbolism than purpose.[4]

---

[4]Stroberg, Mark. Personal Interview, March 2013.

Chapter 8

Medicinal Fried Chicken

"Medicinal Fried Chicken" starts out with the boys at soccer practice. They go to Kentucky Fried Chicken afterward for dinner. When they arrive at the *South Park* KFC, they see that something has changed. So Randy goes inside to find out what's happened. The clerk inside tells him that the KFC is now a marijuana store. Randy is surprised that anyone would sell marijuana openly in public, but the clerk tells him that it's been legalized in Colorado. Randy gets excited and tries to buy marijuana but can't since he doesn't have a prescription.

In another related event, KFC has become outlawed in the entire state of Colorado. This sends Cartman over the edge, who has an addiction to KFC. Cartman becomes part of the illegal KFC black market in *South Park*.

Meanwhile, Randy gives himself cancer so that he can finally get a prescription for medicinal marijuana. The episode ends with marijuana being recriminalized and KFC decriminalized.

Drugs Are Bad, M'Kay?

In this episode, Colorado has passed a law that legalizes medicinal marijuana. Randy is ecstatic about this new law and tries to purchase marijuana at the new marijuana dispensary. He can't, however, since the marijuana is only for patients who have a doctor's recommendation. He goes to extreme lengths to give himself cancer and ultimately gives himself testicular cancer by putting his balls in the microwave. He could just have easily told his doctor that he had chronic back pain.

Should marijuana be legalized? The Libertarian Party has become well known for its stance on drug legalization, and some people believe that legalizing marijuana is the Libertarian Party's primary issue. This is far from the truth. Libertarians simply believe that people have the right to use drugs and that drug use is a victimless crime.

The drug opponents will of course say that drug use isn't a victimless crime. They'll say that people who use mind-altering drugs like marijuana and cocaine put everyone around them in danger. It is true that such drug use will alter one's perceptions. But is the alternative of prohibition any better? If we've learned anything from the prohibition of alcohol, it's that prohibition does not, and cannot, work, no matter what substance it may be.[1]

The prohibition of alcohol in the 1920s drove the production and consumption of alcohol into the black market. After the prohibition was lifted, consumption of alcohol started to decline, and it has been declining ever since. If the use of drugs like marijuana, cocaine, and heroin were suddenly legalized, the use of those drugs would probably decline as well. I sometimes wonder if

---

[1] Paul, Ron. "Prohibition" *Liberty Defined* (New York: Grand Central Publishing, 2011), 225-230.

the prohibition of something makes people want it more. This is called the forbidden fruit effect.[2]

According to Andre Marrou, America had no drug laws and no drug crime before 1914. Marrou says that using drugs was considered a vice, like smoking ciga-rettes, and that "drugs were so cheap and readily available" that nobody really cared if somebody used them.[3]

The people who want to use illegal drugs will do so regardless of government prohibition. So who does the prohibition actually help? It doesn't help the drug users, and it doesn't help the nonusers who may be affected by the users. So who does it help?

Just as alcohol prohibition created gangsters and helped criminals in the 1920s, the prohibition of drugs today only helps drug cartels get rich. If you want to get rid of drug crimes, legalize all the drugs.

Another thing to consider is whether or not you need the government to protect you from yourself. During the South Carolina Republican debate, Ron Paul asked a very good question to the audience: "How many of you would do heroin if it were legal? Oh no, I need the government to tell me not to!" Do you need the government to tell you not to use drugs?

Milton Friedman believes that certain drugs, like crack, would never have existed were it not for the prohibition of marijuana. The prohibition of marijuana, which was easy to interdict according to Friedman, drove people to try other harder drugs like cocaine. He also says that drug prohibition causes on average 10,000

---

[2] Marrou, Andre. "Andre Marrou, Libertarian Candidate for President, 1992. Interview part 2 of 2." http://www.youtube.com/watch?v=wAiDZGwzkXI

[3] Marrou, Andre. "Andre Marrou, Libertarian Candidate for President, 1992. Interview part 2 of 2." http://www.youtube.com/watch?v=wAiDZGwzkXI

homicides a year. To view the whole interview, go to the URL in the footnote.[4]

If you're still not convinced that legalizing drugs will benefit our society, let me tell you about my time in Amsterdam. When I was working in France, I took a three-day trip to Amsterdam. I took three tours of the city: a general tour, a tour of the Red Light District, and a tour of all the marijuana establishments. Amsterdam has a soft drug policy. That means that drugs like marijuana, hemp, and other varieties of cannabis are allowed to be used in designated areas, like coffee houses. Other drugs, like heroin and cocaine, are considered hard drugs and are also illegal.

How can Amsterdam be safe if marijuana is legal and with so many coffee houses? According to the tour guide, Amsterdam is one of the five safest cities in the world. That's right, the world. The other four safe cities were small towns in Sweden. Amsterdam is a good example of how drug legalization does not endanger its citizens.

Toward the end of "Medicinal Fried Chicken", the cashier at the medicinal marijuana dispensary suggests that they simply do away with medicinal marijuana and legalize it since everyone is abusing the medicinal marijuana system.

---

[4]Friedman, Milton. "Why Drugs Should Be Legalized" https://www.youtube.com/watch?v=nLsCC0LZxkY

Finger-Licking Illegal

As one substance starts to become legal (marijuana), another substance starts to become illegal. In this case, it's fatty food. The same liberals who want to legalize marijuana for its health benefits also want to ban restaurants like Kentucky Fried Chicken because they use trans-fat in their shortening.

This particular issue is about freedom of choice, which is discussed in *Butt Out*. Liberals say that fatty foods make people obese and cause heart problems, and therefore should be outlawed. Do people really need a government ban on this type of food to know that it's unhealthy? Is it the government's responsibility to control your eating habits? Should the government mandate gym memberships? Where does it end?[5]

---

[5]Paul, Ron. "Prohibition" *Liberty Defined*, (New York: Grand Central Publishing, 2011), 225-230.

Chapter 9

Die Hippie Die

This episode begins with Cartman going door to door, looking for and eradicating parasites: hippies. This is one of the rare episodes where Cartman is the voice of reason.

Cartman notices an increase in the hippie population of *South Park* and decides to find out why. A group of hippies arrive from the University of Colorado and talk to Stan, Kyle and Kenny about their anti-corporation lectures from college. Cartman eventually concludes that the hippies are preparing a hippie jam music festival, the largest one ever assembled. The mayor tells Cartman that she signed the permit to allow the hippies to have their music festival so they could pump some money into the economy. Cartman tells her that hippies, of course, don't have any money.

While Cartman is in jail for imprisoning a herd of hippies in his basement, more and more hippies arrive and take over the town. The people of *South Park* see no other alternative but to let Cartman out of prison so he can help get rid of them.

His plan is to drill through the hippie crowd and play a Slayer CD on their speaker system. According to Cartman, hippies hate death metal. And his plan works.

Liberal Brainwashing

According to the commentary of this episode, Stone and Parker learned to hate hippies in college. It appears, although they don't flat out say it, that they believe college students are brainwashed into believing liberal ideology.

This is clearly seen when the "college-know-it-all" hippies arrive in *South Park* and tell the boys (except Cartman) that they shouldn't be selling magazines because it helps the giant corporations make money. And they base all their knowledge on one semester of college. And their knowledge is also based on lectures from professors who have probably never been employed in nor have managed a business. So what could they possibly know about corporations?

It's no secret that most college professors are liberal. I read an article in the *Washington Post* that 72 percent of professors identify themselves as liberals.[1] It is also true that many of them teach their students to believe in liberal ideology. Many of the young and impressionable students begin to believe in liberal ideology, and they arrogantly use their education or degree as proof that liberal ideology is right when they argue or discuss economics with conservatives or libertarians. To be fair, I have had liberal professors who were very objective and did not try to impose their views on their students.

The hippies in this episode seem to think that having a rock concert will tear down corporations. But they are not accomplishing anything. All they're doing is smoking pot and jamming to music. Stone and Parker say that there's nothing wrong with smoking pot and

---

[1] Kurtz, Howard. "College Faculties A Most Liberal Lot, Study Finds," *Washington Post*, March 25, 2005. http://www.washingtonpost.com/wp-dyn/articles/A8427-2005Mar28.html

jamming to music. But you need to acknowledge that what you are doing is smoking pot and jamming to music. You are not accomplishing anything by doing so. They should not confuse activity with accomplishment. The hippies also accuse the corporations of being greedy and selfish. But the hippies are just as greedy and selfish as the corporations are. The hippies believe, presumably, that education and other things should be free. How is that not selfish and greedy? And can you name one country in the world that doesn't run on greed?

Chapter 10

ManBearPig

At first, I wasn't going to include this episode in this book. But I decided to after all because it is a fan favorite.

"ManBearPig" begins in the school gymnasium where the guest speaker, Al Gore, has arrived to discuss the single greatest threat to human existence: ManBearPig! ManBearPig is an obvious allegory to global warming. Al Gore tells the school the dangers of ManBearPig and proceeds to try to hang out with the boys, because he apparently has no friends.

Stan feels sorry for him and agrees to attend his ManBearPig meeting. At the meeting, his ManBearPig alarm goes off, and he and the boys go to Cave of the Winds to kill ManBearPig once and for all.

There is, of course, no ManBearPig. Gore's antics gets the boys trapped in a cave where they get stuck for days. They eventually get out and denounce Al Gore as a loser.

I'm Super Cereal!

Some libertarians believe in global warming, and some don't. It's very clear from this episode that Stone and Parker are libertarians who don't believe in global warming. One prominent libertarian who does believe in global warming is Gary Johnson.

Johnson discussed this during a Libertarian Party debate with Lee Wrights. Although he believes that there is evidence of global warming, he acknowledges that the government can't do anything about it. He also says that it might be ten degrees hotter in one government report and twenty degrees hotter in another. Paul also points out that government cannot "plan weather patterns for decades."[1]

---

[1] Paul, Ron. "Global Warming" *Liberty Defined*, (New York: Grand Central Publishing, 2011), 133-143.

Chapter 11

Sexual Harassment Panda

Apparently, this episode has been voted as one of the least favorite episodes among fans, if not the least favorite. In this episode a mascot called Sexual Harassment Panda is the guest speaker for the boys' class.

The Panda tells them what constitutes sexual harassment and even tells them what legal actions they can pursue if they are sexually harassed. This results in an explosion of sexual harassment lawsuits in *South Park*, first between individuals, then between individuals and the school board, and eventually among everybody.

By this point, Sexual Harassment Panda has been living in a commune for misfit mascots. But the boys convince him to use his "panda powers" to convince the people of *South Park* to stop suing one another. And he succeeds.

Taxes Make Me a Sad Panda

Kyle's dad, Gerald, is the lawyer who is representing several people in sexual harassment lawsuits. Gerald is able to help Cartman sue the school for $1.3 million. Kyle asks his dad where the money comes from. Gerald tells him that everyone pays taxes, which go to schools, and that's where he was able to get the money. And of course, Kyle says, "You don't see a problem with that?" But Gerald is either unable or unwilling to explain this, presumably because he knows he's making too much money.

It took me some time to realize what taxes really were: theft. Paying taxes has become such a normal part of life that we don't even realize there was a time when Americans didn't pay income taxes. The income tax was not established until 1913 under the Sixteenth Amendment.[1]

So the income tax is authorized under the Constitution. But does that make it right? Taxation, no matter how you look at it, is theft. I often hear my liberal friends say that the rich should pay more in taxes so the rest of us will benefit from it, and therefore we should vote for the Democratic candidate who will impose higher taxes on the rich.

If you're a liberal reading this right now, ask yourself this: Are you willing to go into a rich person's home and steal their money or possessions? If your answer is no, why would you vote for someone who would steal that person's money on your behalf? If your answer is yes, you are just a common thief.

---

[1] Paul, Ron. "Taxes" *Liberty Defined*, (New York: Grand Central Publishing, 2011), 280-284.

Isn't That Fascism?

Later in the episode, Gerald tries to explain sexual harassment laws to Kyle. He tells Kyle that we live in a liberal Democratic society where Democrats make laws concerning what we're allowed to say and do in the workplace. Kyle says, "Isn't that fascism?"

Then Gerald says it wasn't fascism because we don't call it fascism.

It may not be called fascism, but it is. Liberalism is left-wing fascism, and conservatism is right-wing fascism. Or as Andre Marrou said in an interview with Larry King, "Clinton is a left-wing socialist, and Bush is a right-wing socialist."[2]

Both liberals and conservatives want to limit free speech in some way. As I wrote in *Goo-Backs*, liberals want to enact laws that mandate politically correct speech, and conservatives want to enact laws that mandate English as the only acceptable language. Both are fascist notions.

---

[2]Marrou, Andre. "Andre Marrou, Libertarian Candidate for President, 1992. Interview part 1 of 2." http://www.youtube.com/watch?v=HqMhWHxF_ko

There's No Such Thing As a Free Puppy

Nothing is free! I have heard this from my father so many times during my life. Sexual Harassment Panda tells the audience that there is no such thing as free money. Free market economists usually use what is called the free lunch myth[3] to explain why nothing is free, but this is not as popular as another phrase that my father and many other fathers have said to their children:

There is no such thing as a free puppy!

My father explained to me and my brother that puppies weren't free after having told him that we could get a free puppy from somebody. He explained to us that the person breeding the puppy had to pay in order to take care of the puppy and also had to pay to take care of the puppy's parents. If we received the puppy, he and my mother would be paying for it. They would have to pay for its food, its veterinary bills when necessary, and other dog-related items.

Liberals often speak of free education. Education isn't free; it costs money. What liberals mean to say is that a person's education is being subsidized by those who are not receiving an education. Who is actually paying for this free education? The taxpayers are. Liberals also believe that teachers should be paid more. But where will the extra money come from if the education is free?

I eventually came to the conclusion that education is not a right. Education and healthcare are services that somebody else provides. If you believe that such services are rights, you also believe that someone else

---

[3]Pasour, E.C. "The Free Lunch Myth," May 1, 1978. http://www.fee.org/the_freeman/detail/the-free-lunch-myth#axzz2nXdGr0Aw

must provide you with that service at the expense of someone other than yourself. Do you believe that taking something from someone else without their consent for your own benefit is just? Don't confuse the right to have with the right to pursue. You have every right to pursue such services, but you don't have the right to have them.

Chapter 12

Hooked On Monkey Phonics

This episode begins with the students of *South Park* Elementary competing in a spelling bee. And this year two home-schooled students are also competing, who demonstrate that they have superior spelling skills and eventually win the spelling bee.

Cartman ends up being home-schooled, and Mark, the home-schooled boy, decides that he wants to attend public school so that he can socialize with the other children. Mark eventually achieves his goal of being socially accepted by the other children after he beats up Kyle for having turned his sister into a slut.

The episode concludes with the boys' fathers duct taping the home-schooling father to a flag pole.

Screw You Guys! I'm Going Home-School!

Stone and Parker insinuate that public schools are inefficient but believe that children need public schools to learn social skills. They show how a child can become socially awkward through Rebecca, the home-schooled girl.

While there are home-schooled children who don't learn social skills, it doesn't mean that all home-schooled children are socially awkward. I've met a few people in college who were home-schooled, and I didn't even know that they were home-schooled until they told me.

The inefficiencies in public schools aren't the only problem. According to Robert Kiyosaki, public schools produce good, mindless, obedient employees. They don't produce employers. After reading that, it made me realize that virtually everybody in public schools is preparing their students to enter the workforce. I don't remember any teacher or guidance counselor telling me how I could become an employer.[1]

After attending a home-schooling convention where Ron Paul was a keynote speaker, I learned that there are more reasons to be in favor of home-schooling. According to Paul, many volunteers on his staff who understood what the Constitution meant were home-schooled. He also stated that, since the government controls the public schools, it has no desire to teach the students about the Constitution.[2]

---

[1] Kiyosaki, Robert. *Rich Dad Poor Dad.* (Scottsdale, Arizona: Plata Publishing)
[2] Paul, Ron. *The School Revolution*, (New York: Grand Central Publishing, 2013)

Chapter 13

Mr. Hankey the Christmas Poo

This episode was the first episode of *South Park* I ever watched. This classic episode begins with the children in Mr. Garrison's class rehearsing for a Christmas play for the school. Shelia, Kyle's mother, sees her son playing Joseph and gets infuriated by it. She gets more infuriated when, after telling Mr. Garrison that their family doesn't celebrate Christmas, Mr. Garrison tells her that she shouldn't be raising her child to be a pagan.

Shelia eventually ends up getting the entire town to express their need to not be offended by religious displays in public buildings. Kyle tells everybody about Mr. Hankey, but nobody ever sees him but Kyle, leading others to believe that Kyle is imagining him.

The episode ends with everyone in town believing in Mr. Hankey and singing the iconic *South Park* Mr. Hankey song.

Right Not to Be Offended

Many people nowadays believe that they have the right to not be offended. This notion is preposterous. It would be impossible to not offend one group without offending another. What may be inoffensive to you may be offensive to another.

The show *South Park* itself is offensive to many people. A conservative group called the Parents Television Council has condemned both *South Park* and *Family Guy* for their portrayals of Christianity and Jesus Christ. The PTC has also criticized these two shows of being harmful to child development. The PTC even gives Worst Episode of the Week awards. The PTC, along with other groups, has tried to get both of these programs taken off the air.[1]

Although the creators of *South Park* and *Family Guy* most likely don't agree with each other on most things, they do agree with each other on one thing: If you don't want your children to watch such programs, don't let them. It is not the responsibility of the PTC to decide what others are permitted to watch. If certain television programs offend you, don't watch them. If certain books offend you, don't read them. Nobody is forcing you to watch these programs.

---

[1] "Visit the Parents Television Website and see for yourself." http://w2.parentstv.org/Main/

Chapter 14

The Death Camp of Intolerance

Mr. Garrison is reassigned to teach fourth grade after having taught kindergarten for a while. He's ecstatic to return to teaching older kids, even after he's publicly announced that he's gay. He learns from the school principal that he could sue the school if he were fired for being gay. After hearing this and how much money he could win, he decides to get himself fired for being gay.

When he enters the classroom, he brings his new boyfriend along, Mr. Slave. He uses Mr. Slave to express his homosexuality in front of the children. The children get uncomfortable around them and decide to tell their parents about it. Instead of seeing what Mr. Garrison was doing, the parents decide to teach their children to be tolerant. Mr. Garrison escalates his homosexuality a little more each time in hopes of getting fired. When the children refuse to attend his class, the school recommends sending them to Tolerance Camp.

The episode ends with Mr. Garrison explaining to the parents that there is a difference between tolerating and accepting, and that his behavior was unacceptable for a teacher. The principal doesn't fire him and sends him to Tolerance Camp.

Intolerance Will Not Be Tolerated

Liberals tend to favor laws that forbid social intolerance, while conservatives tend to oppose them. The most recent set of social tolerance laws were the civil rights laws of the '60s. Conservatives oppose such laws on the grounds that they violate private property rights. Libertarians also oppose such laws for the same reason as the conservatives. The opposition of such laws entices liberals to accuse conservatives and libertarians of being racist, sexist, or any other –ist.

Nothing could be further from the truth. Libertarians can't be racist or sexist because we don't put people in such groups. We don't believe in women's rights, gay rights, or any other group's rights. We believe that people get their rights as an individual.

This episode shows that liberals believe that people should accept how others live their lives. At the end of the episode, Mr. Garrison finally tells everyone that there is a difference between tolerating and accepting something. This is the libertarian point of view on such matters. You don't have to agree or even like how someone lives his life, but you don't have the right to tell him that he can't. For example, you may disagree vehemently with homosexuality and same-sex couples, but you don't have the right to tell such people that they can't live that way. All you can do is tolerate it.

What about the laws that say restaurants and other businesses must serve anyone who comes in? Surely, these laws must be fine.

These laws, however, are really no different from the anti-smoking laws that many non-smokers try to pass. It is a violation of private property rights. Let's use a recent example. In the mid 2000s, a bar owner in Philadelphia put a sign on his front window that said that all customers must speak English if they want to enter. I remember clearly that liberals denounced him as being an ignorant xenophobe and thought he was infringing on the rights of free speech. Liberals would love to pass a law saying that he wouldn't be allowed to do that.

Let's examine this a little further. Would a new law make the owner any less xenophobic? Would he still not want to ban all non-English speakers? And would non-English speakers actually want to give this person their business?

Let's use another example. If Joe Barowner were racist against blacks, would you want to give him your business knowing that he was racist against blacks? If Joe were mandated to allow anyone to enter his bar, it doesn't change the fact that he's racist against blacks. If you were black, would you want to give this man your business? Instead of passing legislation that tries to prohibit racism, you can show your opposition by not giving such people your business. This is called *voting with your wallet*.

Chapter 15

Reverse Cowgirl

This episode begins with Clyde's mother scolding him for leaving the toilet seat up. His mother even comes into his class to make him go home and put the toilet seat down. His mother then dies from falling into the toilet bowl.

This death prompted the creation of the Toilet Safety Administration (the TSA). The TSA's duty is to install safety belts on all toilets, regulate restrooms, and eventually monitor restrooms with surveillance cameras.

While the people of *South Park* adjust to the TSA's intrusion in their lives, Kyle and Stan take Clyde to a lawyer, believing that they can receive compensation from the death of Clyde's mother.

The episode ends with the lawyer trying to sue the ghost of the toilet's inventor. His spirit shows up and tells everyone that they're using his invention incorrectly.

Last Bastion of American Freedom

This episode treats the TSA with all the seriousness it deserves. The Toilet Safety Administration is trying to protect people from themselves by installing safety belts to toilet seats and regulating other items in the restroom. The Toilet Safety Administration is present in restrooms and in restaurants, where people have to wait in line and be inspected before they are allowed to use the facility. The nanny state is in full swing here. As Cartman so eloquently put it, toilet time is the last bastion of American freedom.

This episode shows how liberals try to protect people from themselves. I remember a time when wearing seatbelts in cars wasn't mandatory. Is it really anybody's responsibility but your own to make such a decision?

This episode revisits lessons learned in "Butt Out". We can see the tyranny of the majority, freedom of choice, individual responsibility, and the violation of private property rights. Your car is your property, so what right does the government have to tell you to wear your seatbelt? You're not putting anyone's life in danger by not wearing it.

You Can Always Sue Somebody!

Instead of taking responsibility for their own negligent behavior, Randy and the rest of *South Park* decide to sue the inventor of the toilet. But since the inventor has been dead for centuries, they have to summon the ghost of Sir Harrington in a "sue-ance."

This particular scenario has happened several times (not the "sue-ance" part, of course). Somebody gets injured from using a machine or a product incorrectly, so they decide to sue either the inventor or the manufacturer. The amount of frivolous lawsuits could fill an encyclopedia collection.

The most famous frivolous lawsuit of all time was the "McDonald's Hot Coffee Lawsuit." A woman spilled hot coffee in her lap while trying to add cream and sugar. She was eventually awarded $640,000. And that's why McDonald's now has to put caution labels on their cups.[1] I've also heard or read cases of people suing tobacco companies because they got cancer from smoking, people suing fast food restaurants for their obesity, and I've even read a case where a woman tried to sue McDonald's for turning her into a prostitute.[2]

---

[1] H, Christina. "6 Famous 'Frivolous Lawsuit' Stories That Are Total B.S." *Cracked* http://www.cracked.com/article_19150_6-famous-frivolous-lawsuit-stories-that-are-total-b.s..html

[2] Watson, Leon. "McDonald's turned me into a prostitute: Woman's bizarre claim in lawsuit against burger joint" *Daily Mail* http://www.dailymail.co.uk/news/article-2122586/

Chapter 16

Douche and Turd

This episode begins with the People for the Ethical Treatment of Animals demonstrating their opposition to the use of a cow as a mascot for South Park Elementary. Since South Park Elementary can no longer use animals as mascots due to PETA's complaints, they must now choose a new mascot. The boys, however, don't like the choices for mascot and decide to write in their own mascots.

Kyle wants everyone to write in Giant Douche as their new mascot, while Cartman wants everyone to write in Turd Sandwich. Kyle and Cartman believe their mascots to be funnier and better than the others.

The episode proceeds with Giant Douche and Turd Sandwich debating with each other in a presidential debate style. Each of them basically says why it stinks less than the other.

Stan decides that he's not going to vote, because he doesn't like having to choose between a Giant Douche and a Turd Sandwich, as he believes neither of them is any good. Everyone in South Park ridicules him for not taking the responsibility of voting. So they exile him from South Park.

He returns to South Park and decides to vote, but since the PETA members had been killed by this point in the episode, the school decides to go back to the former mascot of the Cow once again.

The Two-Idiot System

"Douche and Turd" shows Stone and Parker's frustration with the current two-party system in America. In an interview for MovieWeb, Parker said that he and Stone are middle-ground guys and that they're sick of people believing that you either have to support Michael Moore or be a right-wing Christian.[1]

I think many Americans, and citizens of other countries where there is a two-party monopoly, feel the same as Stone and Parker do. After my six-month stay in France and seeing the result of voting for the lesser of two evils, I didn't want to vote for Democrats anymore, since I no longer agreed with their economic policies. But I didn't want to vote for Republicans, because they were socially intolerant. I eventually discovered the Libertarian Party.

Another problem with the two-party system is that people will find an issue that they feel very passionate about in one party's platform and then make themselves believe the rest. For example, many people vote Republican because they are pro-life. They may not agree with the rest of the Republican Party's platform at first, but they will convince themselves that they do.

If you decide that you don't want to vote for the lesser of two evils, there will be people who will tell you that you are wasting your vote. But consider this: Unless you live in a swing state like Ohio, where neither the Republicans nor the Democrats have a stronghold, your vote doesn't really make a big difference. For example, if you're a Democratic voter in Kentucky or Texas, your vote is wasted. We all know that the Repub-

---
[1] "Trey Parker and Matt Stone talk Team America: World Police" *MovieWeb* http://www.movieweb.com/news/trey-parker-and-matt-stone-talk-team-america-world-police

lican presidential candidate will win these states. The same is true for Republican voters living in California or Connecticut.

In fact, Peter Schiff, a businessman from Connecticut, said in an interview with Gary Johnson that he has voted Libertarian several times because he knows that his state will vote predominantly Democrat. If Romney and Obama were polling neck and neck in Connecticut, he said he would be more inclined to vote for Romney, but not because he likes Romney. He dislikes Obama so much that he would ignore his conscience and vote for Romney.[2]

You may dislike the two-party system in America, but you know you can always vote for a third-party candidate if the two mainstream candidates don't represent your interests. In France, however, the voting process is different. They use a run-off system, where the candidate with the most popular votes wins the presidency. When I explain this to my friends and family, they immediately think it's a good idea compared to the American system. But the French system isn't flawless. There are two rounds of voting. In the first round, they vote for their candidate. If no candidate receives 51 percent of the popular vote, the top two candidates from the first round go on to the second round. The candidate who wins the majority of the popular vote becomes President.

Does this system sound good to you? It might at first glance, but if you look at the election results of the 2002 French presidential election, you might change your mind. The problem with this system is that you are literally forced to choose between a Giant Douche

---

[2] Johnson, Gary & Schiff, Peter. "Peter Schiff Interviews Gov. Gary Johnson (2012-07-05)" http://www.youtube.com/watch?v=IcwSFsYtBqM

and a Turd Sandwich. In the second round, there is no third option. Typically, the two candidates in the second round are from the Socialist Party and the Union for a Popular Movement (more or less the capitalist party). In the 2002 election, however, the top two candidates in the second round were Jacques Chirac and Jean-Marie Le Pen. Chirac was the (more or less) capitalist candidate, and Le Pen was the candidate of the National Front, a radical right-wing party. Chirac won in a landslide with 82 percent of the popular vote.

The system in the United Kingdom has its flaws as well. British voters don't actually vote directly for the Prime Minister. They vote for their Member of Parliament, and the party that wins the most seats in parliament appoints its leader as the Prime Minister. If the party doesn't win enough seats to form a government, that party has to form a coalition government with another party. In the 2010 general election, the Conservative Party won the most seats, but they had to form a coalition government with the Liberal Democrats. That means that the leader of the Conservative Party is the Prime Minister and that the leader of the Liberal Democrats is the Deputy Prime Minister. This would be like having a Republican President with a Democratic Vice-President. In other words, the British have to deal with both a Giant Douche and a Turd Sandwich at the same time.[3]

I named this section "The Two-Idiot System" after watching a clip from a British satire show called *Spitting Image*. In this clip, they showed Labour and Conservative Members of Parliament arguing with each other. Eventually, a man from a third party stated that the mindless debate between the two major parties

---

[3]Hemsley, Nigel. Personal Interview, March 2013.

strengthened the argument for a third party. But the two major parties did agree on one thing:[4]

The two-idiot system is here to stay!

---

[4]You can view that clip here: "The Two Party System," *Spitting Image* http://www.youtube.com/watch?v=3TFx9u1t1LY

Chapter 17

Other Issues

I'm Super! Thanks For Asking!

In the episode "Cripple Fight", Big Gay Al has been transferred to the South Park wing of the Mountain Scouts. The boys are excited that he's their new scout leader, but the boys' parents are concerned about his homosexuality. The Mountain Scouts receive too many letters from concerned parents and decide to kick him out of the Mountain Scouts. The Mountain Scouts, an obvious reference to the Boy Scouts, has a policy that prohibits homosexuals from being in their organization.

The boys dislike their new scout leader, who happens to be a pedophile by the way, so much that they fight to end homosexual discrimination in the Mountain Scouts. They succeed, but Big Gay Al tells the boys that freedom is a two-way street. If he's free to express his homosexuality, the Mountain Scouts must also be free to express their opposition to homosexual members. The only thing he can ethically do is persuade them to allow homosexuals, not force them to think the way he does.

Since the Mountain Scouts are a private organization, they can deny membership to whomever they want.

The issue of same-sex marriage has taken over the country again, and people on Facebook have been updating their profile photo with a pink equals sign to show their support. Liberals are in favor of using government to enforce marriage equality, and conservatives are of course using government to prohibit same-sex marriage. This issue could be resolved easily by getting government *out* of defining marriage. Marriage has traditionally been a religious ceremony, so marriage should be decided by religious institutions.[1]

---

[1] Paul, Ron. "Marriage" *Liberty Defined*, (New York: Grand Central Publishing, 2011), 183-186.

A 42nd Trimester Abortion

There has not been a *South Park* episode that deals with abortion exclusively, but there have been some references to it. In the episode, "Cartman's Mom Is Still A Dirty Slut," Cartman's mother tries to get a 42nd trimester abortion for her son, only to be told that such a late abortion is illegal. Later in the episode she says:

> I should've thought of raising a child before having sex.

I told a cousin of mine, who always votes Republican, that I was supporting Gary Johnson, the Libertarian candidate for president. Instead of denouncing Libertarians like many Republicans would, he was genuinely interested and asked me what the Libertarian platform was. I told him that Libertarians are fiscally responsible and socially tolerant. He then went on a rant that abortions should be mandatory so that we can get rid of *welfare babies* and *food stamp families*.

My cousin doesn't like the social intolerance of the Republican Party, but he certainly misunderstands the concept of libertarianism. Libertarians would oppose anything that is mandatory.

Abortion seems to be the issue that drives a wedge among libertarians. I've heard arguments for and against abortion from both pro-life and pro-choice libertarians. The pro-life libertarians, like Ron Paul, believe that aborting an unborn baby is an act of aggression and force. The pro-choice libertarians, like Gary Johnson, believe that the government should stay out of a woman's body.[2]

---

[2] Paul, Ron. "Abortion" *Liberty Defined*, (New York: Grand Central Publishing, 2011), 1-9.

Now that both sides of the argument have been addressed, I'd like everyone to ask themselves a few questions regarding abortion:

Would outlawing abortion actually stop abortions from taking place?

Would outlawing abortion not force abortions into the black market like illegal drugs are?

Would you rather have a woman get an abortion or have a child that she cannot or will not take care of?

It's Coming Right For Us!

So far, Stone and Parker have not made an episode that deals with gun control. As far as I know, they have not publicly stated their opinion on the matter. There are two possible reasons why:

1. Perhaps they disagree with each other on gun control.

2. They're too compassionate to make such an episode.

Michael Moore interviewed Matt Stone in his documentary *Bowling for Columbine* about the NRA's decision to have its convention in Colorado shortly after the Columbine incident. Stone says that, while they do have the *right* to, they shouldn't because all they're doing is upsetting people.

Given that the show itself is set in Colorado, Stone and Parker probably don't want to upset their Coloradan neighbors with a gun control episode.

Paul states that the gun control movement has lost momentum recently, but there's no reason to believe that it won't be revived. He also points out that disarmament can lead to genocide, as Hitler did during the Holocaust.[3]

---

[3] Paul, Ron. "Gun Control" *Liberty Defined*, (New York: Grand Central Publishing, 2011), 144-146.

Respect My *Authoritah!*

After completing the first draft of this book, I realized that I had forgotten to write a section about authority. Eric Cartman definitely epitomizes the fascist authoritarian who would use his power and authority to impose his way of thinking on other people. In fact, he even said the following in Butt Out:

> He [Rob Reiner] just goes around imposing his will on people. He's my idol.

Liberals are left-wing authoritarians. Conservatives are right-wing authoritarians. Both want to impose their way of thinking on others. We need to remember that the only authority that politicians have over us is the authority that we allow them to have. So, do they really have any *authoritah*?

Chapter 18

Respect My *Libertah!*

I Learned Something Today

What have we learned today? The most recurring libertarian lesson of *South Park* is individual responsibility. We have seen this lesson stated in several episodes, and even the movie. We've also learned that the tyranny of the majority does not outweigh the rights of private ownership, that people should be free to make their own choices as long as they do not use force or fraud against someone else, that liberals and conservatives are fascists, that capitalism is superior to socialism, and that people don't have the right to not be offended.

We've also learned that it is either acceptable to have government interference in our lives or it is not acceptable. There are no special circumstances.

In a libertarian society, a group of socialists could work together and share the wealth, as long as it's voluntary. In a socialist society, however, a libertarian would not be allowed to keep the fruit of his labor.

The last line of defense of a liberal is to say, "Well, you just don't care." I can't stand when I hear this, because I do care. I care about the right things. Libertarians care more about individual responsibility, personal freedoms, and private property rights. Liberal economic policies, as explained in this book, will create more inflation, more debts for our grandchildren, more dependency on the government, and more unemployment. And they'll do all this in the name of compassion.

There exists a place in our country where everyone is treated equally, receives free food, free healthcare, and where the only people who carry guns are guards and the police. This place is called prison.

Take the world's smallest political quiz again to see if your political stance has changed after reading this book:

www.theadvocates.org/quiz

Recommended Reading

Economics In One Lesson, Henry Hazlitt
End the Fed, Ron Paul
The Law, Frédéric Bastiat
Liberty Defined, Ron Paul
The Real Crash, Peter Schiff
The Revolution, Ron Paul
The Richest Man in Babylon, George S. Clason
South Park and Philosophy, Robert Arp (editor)

Libertarian Websites

United States

www.lp.org
www.facebook.com/libertarians
www.facebook.com/libertariansforronpaul
www.facebook.com/bluerepublican

United Kingdom

www.libertarianpartyuk.com
www.facebook.com/libertarianuk

Canada

www.libertarian.ca
www.facebook.com/libertarianCDN
www.facebook.com/partilibertarienCA

New Zealand

www.libertarianz.org.nz

Australia

www.ldp.org.au

CPSIA information can be obtained at www.ICGtesting.com
Printed in the USA
BVOW06s0441230616

453090BV00010B/38/P